ISBN: 979-8-9946337-1-7

EARTHING
FOR EVERYONE

Your Guide to a Grounding Practice

Ana Cristina Bojanini

Illustrations by Valentina Bojanini

"The miracle is not to walk on water, the miracle is to walk on the green earth, dwelling deeply in the present moment and feeling truly alive."

Thich Nhat Hanh

INTRODUCTION

How would your life change if you made time to connect with the Earth?

This is an invitation to begin your earthing practice. At a basic level earthing is just standing barefoot, sitting or laying on the ground for 20 minutes. This simple act opens you to receive the energy of the Earth and recharge.

As you practice earthing, you reconnect with your body and release the emotions and energies that no longer serve you. It gives you the space to receive the light, love, wisdom and gratitude that flow between the Earth and the Universe. In this book, I share the simple steps I follow as a part of my daily earthing practice. You can use these steps as a guide as you begin to explore earthing.

WHAT YOU NEED

The first thing you need to begin your earthing practice is a spot in nature where you can stand, lay or sit. Ensure your skin is in direct contact with the grass, sand, soil, or moss. If you don't have a place to practice earthing, you can still follow the same steps by going for a walk or using your imagination.

Move through this slowly, it should take you about 20 minutes to complete your earthing ritual.

HOW TO PRACTICE EARTHING

I will guide you as you move the Earth's energy slowly from your feet to the rest of your body. It is important to picture every step in your mind to keep yourself focused and improve your mind-body connection. You will repeat several phrases, like a mantra, directing the Earth's energy to light up a specific body part or system. Through the mantra, you will give thanks to each body part or system for what they do for you. I will also prompt you to release energies and emotions that are stored in certain parts of the body, like sadness, grief, fear, anxiety, trauma, anger, stress and worries.

Once you settle into your earthing area, start by releasing into the Earth other people's energies that might be attached to you. Sometimes these energies can be sticky, so you do this step with conviction. Firmly say out loud:

> *"I am releasing all energies that are not mine into the Earth to be absorbed and recycled. Thank you Earth for receiving them."*

Now, imagine the Earth's energy ascending through your feet. Envision your feet and your legs lighting up. Picture all the cells illuminated. Thank all the cells that have completed their life cycle and let them be dissolved and recycled into the Earth. Thank your lower body for giving you freedom of movement and for supporting your body.

Next envision the Earth's energy lighting up your abdomen. Picture all the cells and organs in this area illuminated. Thank all the cells in your abdomen that have completed their life cycle in this area and let them be dissolved and recycled into the Earth.

Thank your reproductive system for all it produces to keep the balance in your body. Your reproductive system is your connection to your ancestors. As you light up this area, release the ancestral trauma stored here. Let the Earth recycle it.

Thank your urinary system for all it does to filter everything that goes through it. As you light up this area, release the fears that are stored here. Let the Earth recycle them.

Thank your digestive system for producing everything needed to metabolize and absorb the nutrients from food and for getting rid of waste and toxins. As you light up this area, release all the stress stored here. Let the Earth recycle it.

Thank your liver and gallbladder for getting rid of toxins and for producing the substances needed for your metabolism. As you light up this area, release the anger and worries stored here. Let the Earth recycle them.

Thank your pancreas and spleen for all they produce to keep the balance in your body. As you light up this area, release the worries and obsessive thoughts stored here. Let the Earth recycle them.

Continue to move up the body. Envision the Earth's energy lighting up every cell in your chest, neck and nose.

Thank your respiratory system for keeping you alive by receiving the oxygen from the Earth, sending it to all your cells and releasing the carbon dioxide. As you light up this area, release all the sadness and grief stored here. Let the Earth recycle it. Thank all the cells that have completed their life cycle and let them be dissolved and recycled into the Earth.

Envision the Earth's energy lighting up every cell in your arms and hands. Thank your arms and hands for giving you freedom of movement. Thank all the cells that have completed their life cycle and let them be dissolved and recycled into the Earth.

Next envision the Earth's energy lighting up your whole body. Thank all the cells that have completed their life cycle and let them be dissolved and recycled into the Earth.

Thank your immune and lymphatic systems which go everywhere in your body for getting rid of all pathogens and toxins to keep you healthy.

Thank your nervous system, including your brain and all your nerves, for all it does to send and receive information so your brain and body can work in unison. As you light up this area, release the trauma stored here.

Thank your spinal column for keeping you upright and moving in unison. As you light up this area, release the stress stored here.

Thank all the glands in your body for producing the hormones necessary to keep your body in balance. As you light up this area, release the stress stored here.

Thank your fascia which surrounds every cell in your body for keeping your cells interconnected and your bones and muscles in the correct position. As you light up this area, release the trauma and stress stored in your fascia. Let the Earth recycle them.

Thank your five senses: vision, hearing, smell, taste and touch for allowing you to enjoy your experience on Earth.

Earth has now charged and illuminated every cell in your body. Imagine yourself as a beam of light which is connected to both the Earth and the Universe, with both of them creating a shield all around you.

In this moment where you are surrounded and protected by the energy of the Earth and the light of the Universe, say the following words:

I release to the Earth and the Universe anything that is weighing me down.

The Earth and the Universe protect me from all negative energies.

I choose love, happiness, health, abundance, awareness and ... (fill in the blank with what you would like to add).

I forgive anyone who has hurt me and I release all these grudges to the Earth and the Universe.

I forgive myself for any pain I have caused myself and anyone else. I release all these guilt to the Earth and the Universe.

With these emotions and energies released back into the Earth, you can now welcome in something new.

Now, imagine your heart receiving light from the Universe and you sending it to someone, to a situation and/or to anything you believe needs light.

Imagine your heart receiving love from the Universe. Feel your heart overflowing with this love and spilling over to someone who needs it or to a situation you feel needs love to flourish.

Imagine your heart receiving wisdom from the Universe. Ask for this wisdom to help you see situations in a different way and to see solutions instead of problems.

Finally, imagine your heart receiving gratitude from the Universe. Send gratitude to specific people, to your family, to the Universe and Earth for all the blessings you get from them everyday.

To close your earthing practice, gently disconnect from the Earth and the Universe, like unplugging a cellphone that's fully charged. Imagine storing the light from the Universe and the energy of the Earth in your heart.

Rub your hands together. Cover your eyes with your warm palms for three deep breaths. Then cover your ears with your palms for three deep breaths.

Then seal the rest of your body by gently patting yourself everywhere. Say thank you to the Earth and the Universe for letting you connect with them and for recharging you.

My wish for everyone who reads this, is to inspire them to start an earthing practice as soon as possible. You will never stop doing it once you begin.

Acknowledgements

This book was made possible by my daughter Valentina's encouragement, knowledge, and talent. She helped me capture the essence of this daily ritual and bring it to life with her illustrations. It was a true labor of love.

www.ingramcontent.com/pod-product-compliance
Lightning Source LLC
Chambersburg PA
CBHW040906120626
46551CB00006B/666